Let's sing

Speed Sounds

Consonants *Ask children to say the sounds.*

f	l	m	n	r	s	v	z	sh	**th**	**ng**
										nk

b	c	d	g	h	j	p	**qu**	t	w	x	y	**ch**
	k											
	ck											

Vowels *Ask children to say the sounds in and out of order.*

a	e	i	o	u

Each box contains one sound but sometimes more than one grapheme.
*Focus graphemes for this story are **circled**.*

Ditty 1 Let's sing

Story Green Words

Ask children to read the words first in Fred Talk and then say the word.

frog   sing   duck

chick   song

Ask children to read the root first and then the whole word with the ending.

let → let's

Red Words   *Ask children to practise reading the word.*

the

Let's sing

Introduction
Do you like singing? In this story lots of animals have fun singing.

the frog can sing

the duck can sing

the dog can sing

the chick can sing

let's sing a song

Ditty 2 Kiss kiss

Story Green Words

Ask children to read the words first in Fred Talk and then say the word.

rug	bath	with	his
duck	quack	cot	kiss

Red Words *Ask children to practise reading the word.*

the

Kiss kiss

Introduction
*Do you have a younger brother or sister? In this story
we meet a baby. Let's see what he likes doing.*

on the rug

ma-ma

8

in the bath with his duck

quack quack

in his cot

kiss kiss

Ditty 3 La-la-la

Story Green Words

Ask children to read the words first in Fred Talk and then say the word.

bang   drum   sing

with   band

Ask children to read the root first and then the whole word with the suffix.

lot → lots   song → songs

Red Words *Ask children to practise reading the words.*

I   the   of

La-la-la

Introduction

Do you play a musical instrument? This is a story about a girl who really likes music.

I can bang the drum

bang bang

I can sing lots of songs

la-la-la

I can sing with the band

Questions to talk about

Read out each question and ask children to TTYP (turn to your partner) and discuss.

Ditty 1

Which animal sings first?

What do the animals do at the end of the story?

What song shall we sing?

Ditty 2

What does the baby have with him in the bath?

What does Mum do before the baby goes to sleep?

What do you like doing at bathtime/bedtime?

Ditty 3

What instrument can the girl play?

What does the girl do in the band?

What musical instrument would you like to play in a band?

Speedy Green Words

Ask children to practise reading the words across the rows, down the columns and in and out of order clearly and quickly.

a	can	on	in
can	on	can	in